Christine Sinclair

by Chelsea Donaldson

Gail Saunders-Smith, PhD, Consulting Editor

CAPSTONE PRESS

a capstone imprint

Pebble Plus is published by Capstone Press,
1710 Roe Crest Drive, North Mankato, Minnesota 56003
www.capstonepub.com

Cataloging-in-publication data is on file with the Library of Congress.
ISBN 978-1-4914-1959-5 (library binding)
ISBN 978-1-4914-1978-6 (paperback)
ISBN 978-1-4914-1991-5 (eBook PDF)
Written by Chelsea Donaldson

Developed and Produced by Focus Strategic Communications, Inc.
Adrianna Edwards: project manager
Ron Edwards: editor
Rob Scanlan: designer and compositor
Mary Rose MacLachlan: media researcher

Photo Credits
Alamy: Action Plus Sports Images, Title Page, Tony Quinn/Icom SMI, cover; Gunter Marx, 5; Christine Sinclair and Portland Thorns, 7; Newscom: Andy Mead / Icon SMI, 13; The Province: Gerry Kahrmann, 9, Colin Price, 11; CP Images: Adrian Wyld, 15; Landov: Mike Blake, 17, Ben Nelms, 19; GetStock: Lucas Oleniuk, 21.

Note to Parents and Teachers

The Canadian Biographies set supports national curriculum standards for social studies related to people and culture. This book describes and illustrates Christine Sinclair. The images support early readers in understanding text. The repetition of words and phrases helps early readers learn new words. This book also introduces early readers to subject-specific vocabulary words, which are defined in the Glossary section. Early readers may need assistance to read some words and to use the Table of Contents, Glossary, Read More, Internet Sites, and Index sections of the book.

Printed in China by Leo Paper Group in 2014
007039LEOF14

Table of Contents

Early Life

Christine Sinclair is a Canadian soccer superstar. She was born June 12, 1983, in Burnaby, British Columbia. Christine comes from a soccer family. Two of her uncles were professional soccer players.

born in Burnaby, BC

1983

Burnaby, BC

As a child Christine loved sports. She joined her first soccer team at just 4 years old. The team was called the Burnaby Burna Bees. She also joined a baseball team.

born in
Burnaby, BC

1983

1987

joins first
soccer team and
first baseball team

Christine as a Burna Bee

Christine was good at both

sports. But at age 11,

she made a tough decision.

She gave up baseball

so she could focus on soccer.

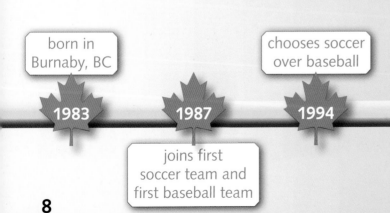

born in
Burnaby, BC

chooses soccer
over baseball

1983

1987

1994

joins first
soccer team and
first baseball team

Christine on a Burnaby girls' soccer team at age 17

Young Adult

Soon Christine was one
of the best young soccer players
in Canada. At just 16 years old,
she joined the Canadian
women's soccer team.

born in
Burnaby, BC

chooses soccer
over baseball

1983

1987

1994

2000

joins first
soccer team and
first baseball team

plays for Canada's
women's soccer team
for first time

Christine (left) playing for the Canadian women's soccer team

A year later a U.S. university offered Christine a soccer scholarship. Christine moved to Portland, Oregon, to go to a university.

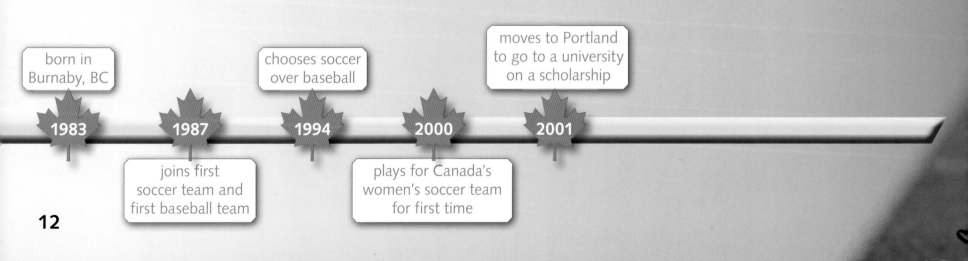

moves to Portland to go to a university on a scholarship

born in Burnaby, BC

chooses soccer over baseball

1983   **1987**   **1994**   **2000**   **2001**

joins first soccer team and first baseball team

plays for Canada's women's soccer team for first time

Christine (right) playing with the Portland Pilots

Christine was a star
on her college team.
In 2002 she was named
the top female college player
of the year. Christine set many
goal-scoring records too.

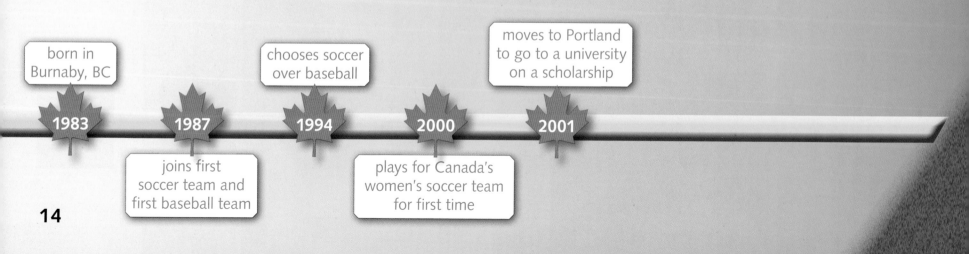

born in
Burnaby, BC

chooses soccer
over baseball

moves to Portland
to go to a university
on a scholarship

1983   1987   1994   2000   2001

joins first
soccer team and
first baseball team

plays for Canada's
women's soccer team
for first time

Christine won the Golden Boot award for scoring the most goals in 2002.

One of the Best

Christine still played for

the Canadian soccer team too.

In 2003 they finished fourth

in the Women's World Cup.

Christine scored three goals.

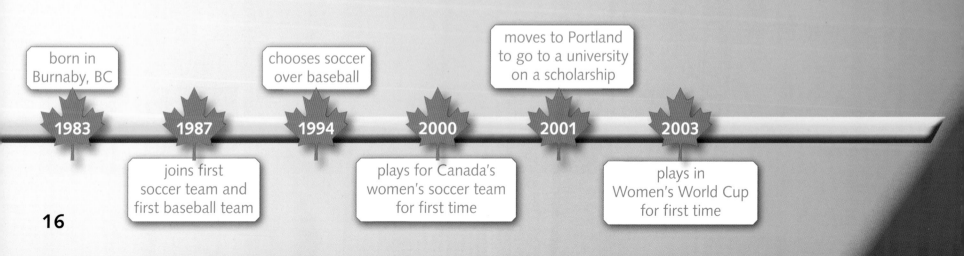

born in
Burnaby, BC

chooses soccer
over baseball

moves to Portland
to go to a university
on a scholarship

1983   **1987**   **1994**   **2000**   **2001**   **2003**

joins first
soccer team and
first baseball team

plays for Canada's
women's soccer team
for first time

plays in
Women's World Cup
for first time

Christine (right) celebrating a goal in 2003

In 2012 the Canadian women's soccer team won medals in the Olympic Games. Christine had become one of the world's best soccer players. But she always gave credit to her teammates.

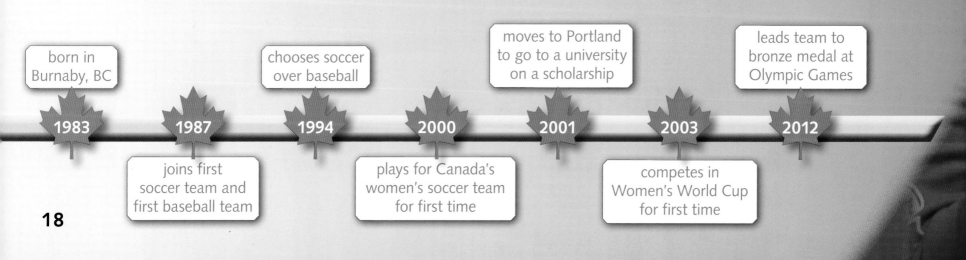

born in Burnaby, BC

chooses soccer over baseball

moves to Portland to go to a university on a scholarship

leads team to bronze medal at Olympic Games

1983

1987

1994

2000

2001

2003

2012

joins first soccer team and first baseball team

plays for Canada's women's soccer team for first time

competes in Women's World Cup for first time

Christine (center) and two teammates at the 2012 Olympic Games

Christine's skills and passion made her a superstar. She has set a great example for young people everywhere.

born in Burnaby, BC

1983

joins first soccer team and first baseball team

1987

chooses soccer over baseball

1994

plays for Canada's women's soccer team for first time

2000

moves to Portland to go to a university on a scholarship

2001

competes in Women's World Cup for first time

2003

leads team to bronze medal at Olympic games

2012

Christine hosting soccer clinics for young girls

Glossary

credit—praise for good work

focus—to place all attention on

passion—to care about something very much

professional—someone who makes money doing
　　something others may do for fun

scholarship—money given to a student to pay for school

Read More

Brodsgaard, Shel and Bob Mackin. *Goals and Dreams.*
A Celebration of Canadian Women's Soccer. Robert's
Creek, BC: Nightwood Books, 2005.

Internet Sites

FactHound offers a safe, fun way to find
Internet sites related to this book. All of the sites
on FactHound have been researched by our staff.

Here's all you do:

Visit *www.facthound.com*

Type in this code: 9781491419595

Super-cool stuff!
Check out projects, games and lots more at
www.capstonekids.com

Index

Word Count: 232
Grade: 1
Early-Intervention Level: 16